GLASS ETCHING

46 Full-Size Patterns with Complete Instructions

GLASS ETCHING

46 Full-Size Patterns with Complete Instructions

Robert A. Capp & Robert G. Bush

Designs by
Robert G. Bush

Dover Publications, Inc., New York

Glass Etching: 46 Full-Size Patterns with Complete Instructions is a new work, first published by Dover Publications, Inc., in 1984.

Library of Congress Cataloging in Publication Data

Capp, Robert A.
  Glass etching.

  1. Glass etching—Patterns. I. Bush, Robert G. II. Title.
TT298.C36 1984   748.6   83-5257
ISBN-13: 978-0-486-24578-2
ISBN-10: 0-486-24578-0

Manufactured in the United States by Courier Corporation
24578017   2014
www.doverpublications.com

INTRODUCTION

A craft whose roots reach back more than three centuries, glass etching is now enjoying great popularity among artists who value the marvelous frosted effects that can be produced on glass with sandblasting and acid-etching techniques. The appeal of glass etching has grown as the basic simplicity of the craft has been more widely discovered. Novices are able to create works of stunning beauty with little instruction; experienced etchers enjoy the great variety of design and decoration options available to them.

This book contains complete instructions for sandblasting and acid-cream etching along with 46 full-size, reusable stencil patterns. The main designs include a cheetah, cockatoo, toucan, Siamese and Persian cats, morning glories, fuchsia, water lilies, roses and other popular subjects. A few selected frame styles are represented with corner and side elements that can be repeated or combined to form complete units.

The glass projects that can be etched are nearly limitless: window and door panes, lamp and mirror panels, mobiles, leaded or framed pictures, shower doors, room dividers, vases, glasses, bottles, plates—even crystal balls. The patterns in this book are best suited to large glass panels, but they can be adapted for smaller projects, too. Most of all, the craft of glass etching requires imagination and the desire to experiment with different effects.

HISTORY

Glass was probably etched for the first time in the late seventeenth century when the Bavarian master craftsman Henry Schwanhart of Nuremberg used a corrosive acid to decorate window panes. The development of the craft was slow, largely because of the toxic fumes released from the vats of hydrofluoric acid in which the glass was immersed while the pattern was gradually etched on the plate. Designs were made on the glass by using wax or resin resists to protect areas of the glass and keep them from being etched. Acid-etched glass reached the height of its commercial success during the Victorian era when mass-produced decorative tableware was extremely popular.

In 1870 a new method of etching was introduced that utilized the abrasive action of a stream of sand shot at a glass surface by air pressure. Durable steel and rubber stencils replaced wax resists. Sandblasting allowed a great variety of depth and detail to be etched on glass in a much shorter time than was needed for acid etching.

Recently, many new products have been developed for etching at home or in small studios. Acid creams and gels now offer quick and painless etching. A wide selection of sandblasting units has also become available. With a little work and attention to detail, home etching results can rival those produced in large glass firms.

INSTRUCTIONS

Acid-cream etching and sandblasting differ in technique, but they share many of the same basic materials and preparation steps. The acid cream used in etching glass is a dilute form of hydrofluoric acid and it produces an even etch on the surface of the glass. Acid-cream etching is quick, simple, inexpensive and can be done in a small space. More equipment and special enclosed or isolated areas are required for sandblasting, but the degree of detail and the variety of effects that can be created with sandblasting are far greater than those that can be obtained with acid cream. Low-priced acid-cream etching kits are available from many sources. Sandblasting can be learned by renting equipment or taking courses at glass-decorating studios.

The instructions in this book are divided into three sections. Section 1 discusses basic etching materials and the equipment necessary for acid-cream etching and sandblasting. Section 2 deals with applying resists onto glass plus transferring and cutting stencil patterns. Etching techniques are described in Section 3.

Following the instructions are stencil patterns, printed on one side of the page only, to allow for easy transferring. Black-and-white illustrations of the designs are included in the stencil section to show the two different parts, etched and unetched, of a design. Many of the patterns are complete as shown, but some can be placed inside frames or repeated and combined with other patterns. The frame sections can be combined in numerous ways to make a variety of attractive borders. The patterns can also be enlarged, reduced, extended or altered to fit your glass more precisely.

Be sure to follow all safety precautions suggested in this book and in the directions to your etching equipment. Injuries can result if proper care is not taken when sandblasting or acid etching. If you follow the basic instructions given in this book, glass etching should be an enjoyable and rewarding hobby.

Section 1. Materials and Equipment

A. Glass

Most local glass dealers stock a variety of colors and thicknesses of glass. Some of the most common types include clear, bronze (brown), smoked (gray), peach and obscure (usually placed in shower doors and bathroom windows). The use to which the glass will be put determines the thickness that is needed, but ¼"-plate glass is generally best. Glass that will be used as a tabletop should be ⅜" or ½" thick. Tempered glass should be used in doors and other areas where there is a greater possibility of breakage. It is approximately ten times stronger than regular glass and shatters into small pieces that are much less likely to do serious harm than the large, jagged pieces created by regular broken glass. Many communities have regulations concerning the glass that can be installed in doorways and similar areas. You should check with your local glass dealer or government building-standards office when such applications are planned.

Mirrors are available not only in clear, bronze, smoked and peach, but also in a variety of antiqued or veined colors. The effects achieved in etching mirrors on their front and back surfaces are somewhat different. Etching on the front of a mirror creates a double or reflective image. A sharp-edged single image is obtained when the back is etched (or the silvering is removed from a section so that a photograph can be inserted). Lettering that is etched on the backs of mirrors should be flopped to read correctly from the front.

Whether working from the front or back of a mirror, extra care should be taken to avoid scratching the glass or silvering. The smallest scratch is visible on a mirror, while it may pass unnoticed on plain glass. Special attention should be given to the angle of the knife when cutting out a stencil on the back of a mirror. A knife that is not held perpendicular to the back of the mirror will cause hairline cuts in the silvered areas that are not being etched.

When the silvering is removed from a mirror and the finished piece is placed either in or near a window opening, the sunlight coming through the etched portions creates a remarkably beautiful glow. The etched design on the back can also be resilvered by spraying or painting it with silver leaf. Gold, bronze and other metallic leafs can also be used to give added color and richness.

Etched areas glitter more when they are professionally silvered; check with your local glass dealer for the locations of such services.

The edges of glass and mirrors can be finished in a variety of ways including swiping, beveling (in widths of ½", 1" and 1½"), pencil polish, flat polish and other specialty polishes. You should have glass and mirror edges at least swiped prior to beginning work. This treatment simply removes the sharp edges and will protect against cuts while handling the glass. A swiped edge does not have a finished look and should be used on pieces that will be inserted in a frame. All edgework should be done before a piece is etched because most glass shops will not guarantee against breakage on a finished piece.

Another type of glass often used by etchers is flashed glass, which most stained-glass dealers carry in a wide variety of colors. Many stained-glass shops incorporate etched flashed-glass pieces in their stained-glass windows. Flashed glass is a layer of clear glass with a thinner layer of colored glass flashed or adhered to it. When the colored layer is etched away, it leaves a frosted, colorless area. When the colored glass is partially etched away, it leaves an area that is frostier and lighter in color than the untouched areas.

The effects that can be achieved with flashed glass are startling. When etching flashed glass, it is important to remember that the colored layer will vary in thickness. Because of the fragile nature of this beautiful glass, special care should be exercised when working with it. Flashed glass should be framed or mounted upon completion.

B. Masking Materials

Many brands of masking materials, vinyl papers and tapes and liquid solutions are available for use as resists. The masking papers come in rolls or sheets that vary in thickness. Ranging from 6 to 30 inches in width, they are available at many hardware and craft stores, home-improvement centers, drugstores and supermarkets.

Two widely used resists are A-21 contact paper and an excellent brand of paper called Buttercut. One layer of A-21 contact paper is usually sufficient for acid-cream etching and single-stage sandblasting. Designs can be drawn on solid-color papers (white is preferable) with either pen or pencil, and all markings are erasable. Clear contact papers can be marked with some types of ink. Stencils can be cut easily on one layer of contact paper. If you are doing deep-etch blasting, however, you will need two or more layers of contact paper, depending on how deep you will be etching. The best choice for deep-etch blasting is Buttercut, which comes in three thicknesses. Thick or multilayered resists quickly dull knife blades, but they are recommended on sandblasting projects until you have gained some experience in etching techniques.

Acid etchers can use liquid resists instead of contact paper. They are available in kits with special etching cream and instructions. Liquid resists are much like old-style wax resists and are especially useful for etching fine detail. After the glass is coated with the transparent resist, it is laid (resist-side up) over a design, which can then be sketched into the resist. (Note: the instructions in Section 2 deal with vinyl-paper resists rather than liquid resists.)

C. Knives

All masking materials dull knife blades fairly quickly. Because the quality of your finished piece depends upon the quality of the cut stencil, it is best to use a sharp blade at all times. A hobby knife with #11 X-ACTO blades is often used since it fits well in the hand and is carried by most hardware and art-supply stores at a reasonable price. Cutting curved lines is very easy with a swivel knife. The blade swivels in the knife handle, allowing you to almost write with the knife. Blades for swivel knives are stocked in fewer stores and are more expensive. Also available are a few brands of adjustable double-bladed knives that allow parallel lines to be cut in a single movement. Double-bladed knives are fairly expensive and many are offered without replaceable blades.

D. Transfer Materials

Pens or pencils, rulers, carbon paper and masking tape are used for transferring a design onto nontransparent, solid-color resists. Carbon paper is not necessary when using a clear resist.

E. Acid Creams

There are many brands of etching cream on the market. Though they are far safer than the undiluted hydrofluoric acid that was once used to etch glass, caution should still be exercised when using modern acid creams. Make sure to follow the instructions that accompany the cream. Plastic or rubber gloves are often necessary. A medium-sized brush or cotton swabs will be needed for spreading the etching cream over the stencil.

F. Sandblasting Equipment

Blasting units. It is not necessary to purchase your own equipment when you first begin experimenting with sandblasting techniques. You should be able to find businesses listed in your local Yellow Pages that will provide sandblasting services for your glass projects.

If you decide to purchase your own equipment, the most costly item will be an air compressor. Run by either a gasoline engine or an electric motor, the compressor supplies the blast of air that forces the sand from a hopper through a hose to a gun and then against the surface of the glass. Low-horsepower air compressors can be purchased at some department stores and through businesses that specialize in sandblasting equipment. Before making a purchase, explain your needs to some local dealers and have them describe the features of the different types of available equipment. The size of the engine or motor, the tank size and the pulley ratio between compressor and engine or motor are just a few of the specifications that directly affect your sandblasting capabilities. Any electric compressor over 2 hp usually requires an electrical source of 220 watts.

Shop around and make sure that you get the right system to meet your needs.

The sandblasting unit consists of a bucket or hopper with a capacity of 5–10 gallons and with a screened top to keep coarse objects from clogging up the system. A hose runs from the bottom of the hopper and attaches to the gun. The air hose coming from the air compressor also attaches to the gun. Complete sandblasting kits or units are available from some department stores and specialized dealers. The quality of your etching greatly depends on the quality of your sandblasting gun, so you may want to buy a better gun than the one that comes with a kit. Quality sandblasting guns are usually only available through specialized dealers.

Blasting booths and safety equipment. As previously mentioned, some glass shops and sandblasting businesses provide individualized services for craftspeople, including renting out sandblasting booths and units. A sandblasting studio is a good place in which to learn about and experiment with sandblasting techniques and equipment.

For those who want to buy sandblasting equipment and set up their own operations, a properly situated and furnished blasting area is a primary consideration. A board or shelf attached to a wall in an out-of-the-way, outdoors area comprises the simplest blasting area. Some communities do not allow outdoor blasting, however; again, you should ask sandblasting businesses or the local government safety-standards board about blasting regulations in your area. Safety precautions must be taken for all methods of blasting.

Sandblasting can be done in either an unenclosed or enclosed booth. Unenclosed booths are shelves or platforms, with or without surrounding side walls, that are set up against a wall in any place where there is no danger of other people being closely exposed to the flying particles and dust created by blasting. This method of blasting is also known as a nonrecovery system because the abrasive sand that is shot against the glass is not trapped and recycled. Much of the spent abrasive falls in a pile under the shelf, however, and if you place a mat on the ground you can sweep up the sand and pour it into the hopper's screened top. A dust mask and goggles should always be worn when blasting in an unenclosed booth.

Working in an unenclosed booth exposes you to dust created by the blasting. If inhaled, the dust can cause the deadly lung disease silicosis. A good dust mask is therefore necessary with nonrecovery systems. You should use a dust mask with a heavy plastic nosepiece into which one or two replaceable filters can be screwed. This type of mask is far more effective than are inexpensive paper filters.

Eyes must be protected with goggles from flying particles, which can cause extreme pain and permanent injury. Select goggles that fit snugly to your head. There are also hoods available that cover and protect the entire upper torso. These hoods are available either with or without air-feed lines. Your local specialized dealer can assist you in making a proper selection.

An enclosed booth, which allows you to stand outside a sealed compartment and blast the glass inside through a hole in a plastic curtain, is a neater and very handy alternative to an unenclosed blasting area. Enclosed booths can be constructed fairly cheaply out of heavy plastic sheets and other materials and set up in basements, garages, sheds and other convenient spots. The booth (6 ft. high by 4 ft. wide by 3½ ft. deep is an average size) can be constructed in a variety of ways; plastic sheets supported by a wood frame or by walls, or a plywood structure with a plastic window in front, are two possible constructions.

Enclosed booths should be well sealed and have a fan and exhaust system that removes from the booth the dust created by blasting and vents it in a safe place. Be sure that the opening to your booth is sealed shut when blasting. The shelf that the glass is set on is attached to the back wall and a small hole is cut in the plastic sheet in front into which the nozzle of the sandblasting gun is inserted when blasting. You may wish to attach a protected light to the inside of the booth.

Enclosed booths are also known as recovery systems because spent abrasive can either be funneled by interior sloping sleeves back into the hopper (placed inside the booth) or swept up off the floor and reused. Wearing goggles and dust masks is not absolutely necessary when using a properly constructed enclosed booth, but you should make sure that all dust in the air has been removed from the booth before opening it after blasting.

A large variety of enclosed commercial or industrial sandblasting booths are usually available through specialized dealers found in your local Yellow Pages. Researching the types of booths available prior to building your own will help you design a booth that meets your specific needs.

Abrasives. The half-dozen or so varieties of abrasive materials used in sandblasting glass come in different grits, or coarseness levels. The texture left on the glass after blasting is determined by the size of the grit used. Generally, large grits produce coarse textures and small grits leave fine textures. The effect that you wish to produce on the glass will influence the type of abrasive and grit level you use. Your selection may be limited by the amount of pressure generated by your sandblasting unit and the bore or width of the nozzle on your sandblasting gun. When buying sandblasting equipment, check to see if particular abrasives or grit levels are recommended.

Grit levels range from 20 to 200 (the lower the grit number, the coarser the abrasive). Grit levels of 60–80 leave a coarse-textured surface and can be used for cutting holes through glass. Medium-weight grits of around the 100 level are good for simple and deep-etch blasting. Fine grits in the 150–200 range are good for producing soft, frosted surface treatments.

Two of the most commonly used abrasives are silica sand and crystal silica. They are inexpensive, but they dull and break down quickly and are best used in a nonrecovery system. Garnet is the next step up from the silica abrasives. It is a little more expensive but doesn't break down as quickly. Aluminum oxide and silicon carbide are the most expensive and long-lasting of the abrasives and are best used in recovery systems. Silicon carbide actually breaks down into sharper particles that can be used over and over.

Section 2. Design and Stencil Preparation

A. Applying the Resist

Before covering glass surfaces with a resist, you should make sure that they are clean. If the glass is not clean, the resist will not adhere properly and the cut stencil may peel up during the etching process.

After determining what type of etching you will be doing and how many layers of masking material you will need, you can apply the resist to the front surface of your glass. Cut a section of masking material that is a little larger than your glass piece. Pull the backing off a little way and stick the resist to one edge of the glass, overlapping the edge by about ½". Continue to pull the backing off, smoothing the resist down on the glass with your hand as you pull. The backing should be peeled off slowly and the resist pressed down firmly so that air bubbles are not trapped under the sheet. If air bubbles appear, poke them with a pin or the tip of your knife and smooth down the resist. If air bubbles are allowed to remain, the resist may break down under the pressure of blasting or acid cream may leak under the resist and cause the glass to be etched in unwanted areas. Once the top of the glass is properly covered, additional resist layers can be applied to the first layer.

If you are using a nontransparent resist, it is better to cover the back of the glass with a resist at the same time that you cover the front. When using a clear resist, do not cover the back of the glass until you have cut out the design on the front resist. Overlapping edges of the front and back resists should be pressed together.

B. Preparing the Design

Some of the patterns in this book may be used as they are, others will need further design work. The patterns can be photomechanically enlarged or reduced and the frames and main designs can be combined. The title page shows one possible combination of design elements using a fish pattern and an Art Nouveau-style frame. Many of the patterns include captions that offer design suggestions. Designs should fit attractively within the edges of your glass piece, with all design elements appearing in proportion to one another and to the size of the glass.

All of the patterns can be flopped to create symmetrically matching designs. To make a flopped image, tape a pattern to a window with the design facing out. Place a sheet of typing paper over the pattern and trace the image. Repeats of original and flopped images (which are often needed in making a frame) can be traced with carbon paper onto other sheets of paper. Once you have all of the flopped and repeated images necessary for a complete design, you can tape the pieces together on one sheet of paper, or transfer them onto the resist, and extend lines to connect frame sections.

The pages with frame elements contain two to four different corner or side designs rather than one complete design. By flopping and repeating a frame corner and extending the lines on the sides of the aligned sections until they meet, you can make a frame of any size and shape. Frames can be used to enclose names, titles, messages and main designs or to highlight a central mirror area.

The self-contained main designs (those which are already enclosed within a frame) can be centered on the glass with the help of guidemarks drawn on the resist and on the design. To make the guidemarks, divide the design into quarters with vertical and horizontal lines through the center. Repeat the quartering lines on the resist that covers the glass. The design can be centered by aligning the guidemarks and can then be taped to the glass.

C. Transferring and Cutting the Design

If you are using a clear resist, you do not have to use a pen and carbon paper to trace your pattern onto the resist before cutting it out. After you have covered the front of the glass with the resist, carefully lay the glass (resist-side up) on top of the design. Secure the glass to the design with tape and proceed to "trace" the design onto the resist with your knife. The clear resist's distracting haze and the distortion produced by the thickness of the glass may cause some initial problems. Take your time cutting the design and you will quickly overcome these slight difficulties. After the entire design has been cut, the pattern should be removed from the back of the glass and replaced by a resist to protect the back side of the glass during the etching process.

If you are using a nontransparent resist, you must transfer the pattern onto the resist before cutting it out. Lay your completed design on top of the resist and center it as described in Section 2B.

Tape the pattern to the resist on three sides and slip a piece of carbon paper between the resist and the pattern with the carbon facing down. Tape the papers securely and trace the entire design onto the resist. Remove the pattern and carbon paper after checking to see that all lines have been clearly transferred.

The design can be cut after it has been transferred onto the nontransparent resist. Be sure to replace knife blades as soon as they become dull. A dull blade will pull the resist away from the glass; the resist may then fall off during the etching process. Take your time when you are cutting. Remember, your finished piece will only be as good as your cut stencil. *Eyeglasses or goggles should be worn while you are cutting the design since the tips of blades tend to break off and fly away when being used on plastics.*

D. Removing Stencil Sections

Once the design has been cut on the resist, you must determine which of the two areas of the pattern you will be etching. A design etched on a clear background creates a very striking effect. If privacy is desired, however, the background can be etched to produce an extraordinarily beautiful effect commonly known as reverse etching. The black-and-white illustrations that appear throughout the book display the etched (black) and unetched (white) stencil sections. The main design is shown in black in the majority of the illustrations. Some of the patterns are shown both ways with colors reversed. The Persian cat and cockatoo are illustrated with the main design in white only—examples of reverse etching. Compare the illustration of the Persian cat with that of the Siamese cat, or the cockatoo with the toucan, and decide whether you prefer the regular or reverse effect for your chosen pattern.

After you have made your choice, remove the resist from the areas that are to be etched. You will probably need to refer to the illustration of the pattern to determine which parts of the stencil should be removed. The cut-out resist sections should be pulled up carefully so as not to mar a clean-cut edge. When all the areas to be etched have been removed, you can etch the glass by using one of the techniques described in Section 3.

For the more advanced sandblasting techniques described in Section 3, the resist is removed from the areas to be etched in different blasting stages. When using these techniques, you may find it helpful to number the resist sections (on a separate sketch) to show at which stage they should be removed.

Section 3. Etching Techniques

A. Acid-Cream Etching

Read the instructions that come with your etching equipment before beginning work. Rubber gloves are required with some creams. Skin and clothes should not come in contact with etching creams. Work surfaces and surrounding areas should be well protected with newspaper. Always work near a water source in a well-ventilated area. An industrial-grade sink or an outdoor water source is best for rinsing off the etched glass since some creams can cause damage to household sinks and tubs.

After the stencil has been cut and the areas that are to be etched have been peeled away, the glass exposed in the cut-out sections should be cleaned with cotton or a lint-free towel (do not use glass cleaner). Oil from your fingertips and adhesive left by the peeled-off resist will act as resists to the acid cream if they are left on the glass.

When the glass is clean, take a brush or cotton swab and apply generous amounts of cream to the glass in the cut-out sections. The cream should be applied slightly beyond the cut-out lines to insure an even etch. Allow the cream to etch the glass for the amount of time recommended on your bottle of cream, usually between 5 and 15 minutes. After the cream has stood long enough, rinse the glass under running water. Be sure to rinse the glass thoroughly so that unetched areas do not get spoiled by drops of residue acid when the resist is removed. When you are satisfied that all the cream has been washed off, remove the resist and give the glass a final cleaning with a mixture of 50% window cleaner and 50% acetone (this can be found in most hardware and paint stores).

B. Sandblast Etching

The effects that can be created on glass by sandblasting are quite varied. Along with the relatively even etch produced by the simple blast method, deep-etch and frost-blasting techniques can be used to give the glass a three-dimensional or textured look. Depending on which method you use, the cut-out stencil sections are removed all at once, in stages or piece by piece. Be sure to follow all safety precautions described in previous sections.

Simple Blasting. Begin by removing the cut-out stencil sections from the areas to be etched. Set the glass firmly in place in its booth and then blast the entire surface of the piece. The distance that you should keep the gun from the glass when blasting is determined by the grit size of the abrasive and the amount of air pressure being used. Generally, a distance of 8–10 inches will give you a fairly uniform etched surface. Different effects can be achieved by selectively etching one area more than another. Do not let your gun get too close to the glass because you may melt or tear the edges of the resist.

After blasting the glass, inspect the design thoroughly to make sure that it has been completely etched. When you are completely satisfied with the etching, remove the resist from both sides of the glass. Rinse the completed piece with running water to wash off any remaining dust and abrasive particles. Finally, wipe both sides of the glass with a 50% window-cleaner/50% acetone mixture.

Deep-Etch Blasting. Interesting highlights can be created by etching some parts of a design more deeply than others. Two types of deep-etching are discussed here. In the first, glass is blasted to different levels so that some features of a pattern become more pronounced. In the second, the etched sections of a pattern are "carved" up by blasting one small area at a time to create a varied surface texture. The level to which the deepest areas of your pattern can be blasted depends on the thickness of your glass. Except for the differences specified below, deep-etch blasting techniques follow the same general procedure as that used in simple blasting.

Multilevel stage blasting allows you to highlight certain sections of a pattern by blasting them more deeply than other sections. You might, for instance, choose to make a cat's eyes and mouth stand out or etch one line in a frame deeper than another. A thick resist should be used. Multilevel stage blasting occurs in two or more steps. The resist is first removed from the sections that are to be etched the deepest, and they are then uniformly blasted. The resist is then removed from the areas that are to be etched second deepest and a second uniform blasting is made. The sections that are etched first will get a little deeper than surrounding areas each time another level is blasted. The completed piece can be viewed from either the front or back.

Deep-etch carving involves blasting small adjoining areas separately to create a larger etched section with a varied surface. With this method, folds in cloth, fish scales, clumps of fur on a cat and bird feathers can be etched so that an overlapping effect is created. Deep-etch carving requires a very thick resist since the gun is held close to the glass when blasting. Because the resist is removed and the glass blasted one area at a time, this technique requires a great deal more time than simple blasting or multilevel stage blasting. Intricate carving can take hours.

First, make a pencil sketch of your design that shows the surface texture that you wish to etch (scales, feathers, etc.). Then, working from your sketch, make a detailed blueprint of your design showing which side of each etched area is to be deep-etched and which side is to be clear or lightly etched. The etched sections of the patterns in this book will usually need to be divided into much smaller areas.

When all preparations have been made, remove and blast the design areas one by one to the desired depth. The gun should be held close to the area you are blasting in order to concentrate the blast. By directing your gun at one side of an area, you can deep-etch one point or side and make the rest of the less deeply etched area fade gradually to the opposite edges.

Frost Blasting. Much like deep-etching, frost blasting concentrates the blast to one side of each etched area. A light blast is used, however, allowing the lightly etched side to "fade" into clear glass on the opposite side of the area. A fine-grit abrasive is used to produce light frosts and shadings. Each area of the design is blasted separately at close range. Again, concentrating the blast to produce a heavier shading on one side and lighter tones or clear glass on the other side of an etched area will create an overlapping effect. Frost blasting can be combined with other blasting techniques. You might, for instance, wish to deep-etch a lily pad and frost-blast the water around it, or deep-etch the feathers on the head of a bird and switch gradually to a frost blast for the body feathers.

Note: To make the patterns easier to use, the back sides of the pages (every other double-page spread) have been left blank.

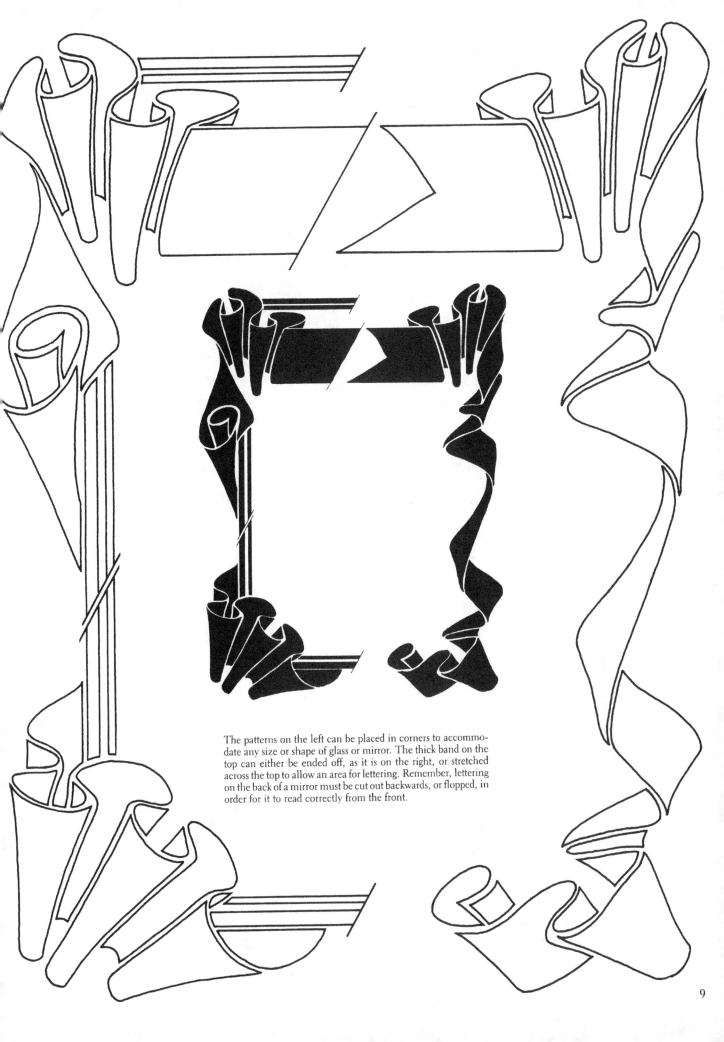

The patterns on the left can be placed in corners to accommodate any size or shape of glass or mirror. The thick band on the top can either be ended off, as it is on the right, or stretched across the top to allow an area for lettering. Remember, lettering on the back of a mirror must be cut out backwards, or flopped, in order for it to read correctly from the front.

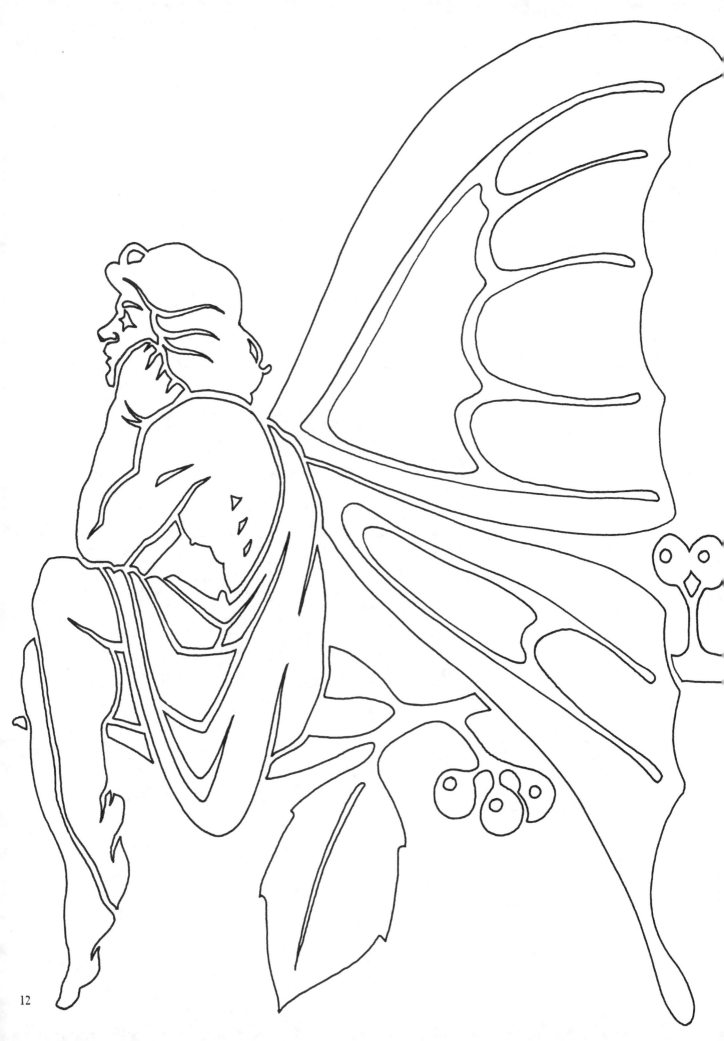

The illustrations on page 16 show the appearance of the two patterns when they are used together. The bottom illustration shows the reverse-etch appearance.

Illustrations of the patterns on pages 12 and 13, showing the regular and reverse-etch appearance.

A very attractive Art Nouveau mirror of any size or shape can be made by using the fish pattern in the bottom corners. The wave pattern can be used as shown, or turned 90° as shown in the center illustration and on the title page.

17

Each of the four different corner patterns can be repeated four times and linked together to fit any size or shape of glass or mirror. A cork-backed metal ruler is your best tool for cutting clean straight edges. The cork keeps the ruler from slipping while cutting out the pattern on the resist. Freehand rounded corners require concentration, patience and practice.

The illustrations inside the frame patterns show the morning glory pattern that appears on the top of page 21 and the grapevine pattern that appears on the top of page 25 (their reverse-etch appearance is shown on page 24). The patterns at the bottoms of pages 21 and 25 feature water-lily designs of complementary shape and size.

See caption on page 20 for design notes.

The two patterns at the top of the page are essentially the same except for the overlapping of one line over the other in the right-hand pattern. Note how the pattern on the left draws your attention toward the corner. You can use overlapping designs to direct attention when creating your own designs. The bottom two patterns illustrate the same concept. The center illustrations show the reverse-etch appearance of the patterns on the top of pages 21 and 25.

Regular and reverse-etch illustrations of the grapevine
pattern at top are shown on pages 20 and 24.

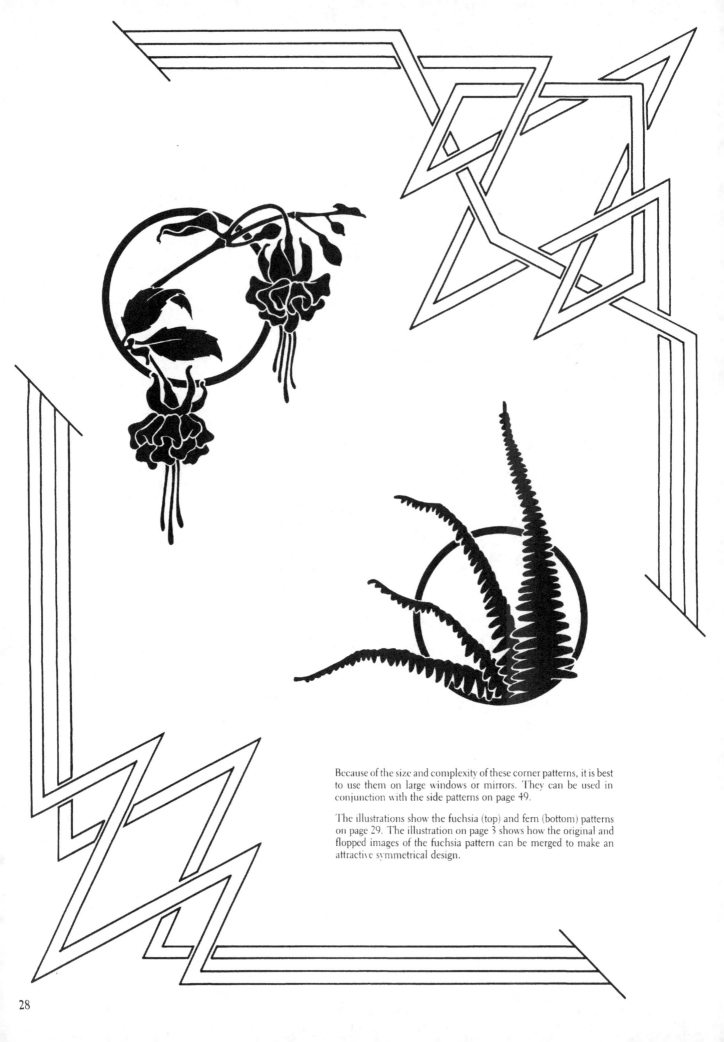

Because of the size and complexity of these corner patterns, it is best to use them on large windows or mirrors. They can be used in conjunction with the side patterns on page 49.

The illustrations show the fuchsia (top) and fern (bottom) patterns on page 29. The illustration on page 3 shows how the original and flopped images of the fuchsia pattern can be merged to make an attractive symmetrical design.

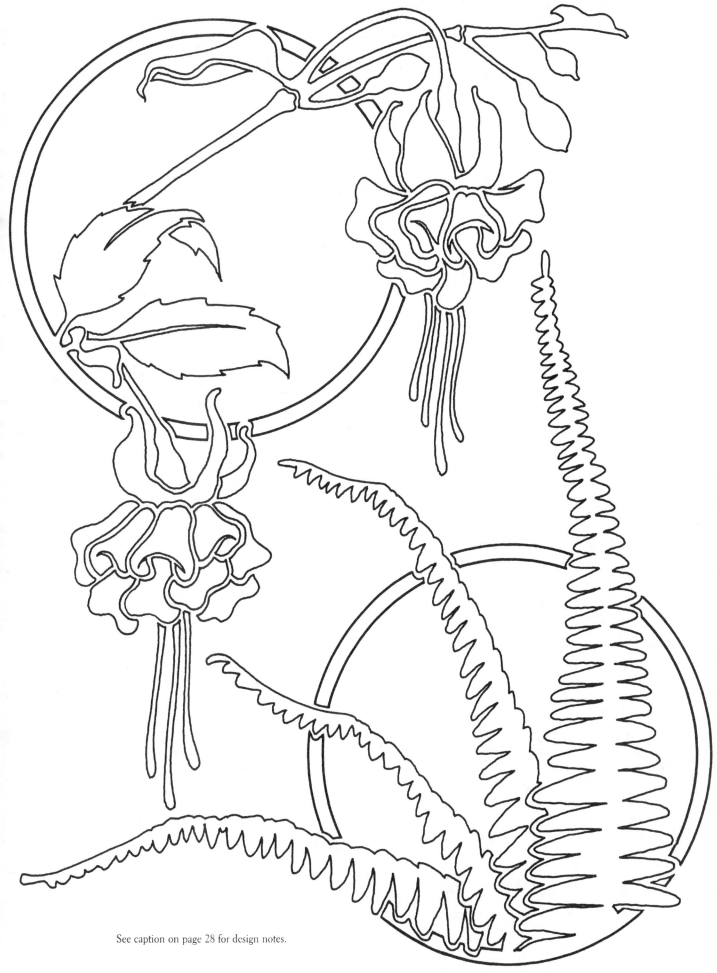

See caption on page 28 for design notes.

An illustration of the cheetah pattern appears on page 40.

An illustration of the Siamese cat pattern appears on page 41.

The illustration on page 41 of the Persian cat pattern shows the reverse-etch appearance. Compare it to the Siamese cat illustration to its left.

An illustration of the pattern on pages 32 and 33.

At top, the reverse-etch appearance of the Persian cat pattern from page 37 can be compared with the illustration of the Siamese cat pattern from page 36. At bottom, the same comparison can be made for the cockatoo pattern from page 45 and the toucan pattern from page 44.

An illustration of the toucan pattern appears on page 41.

The illustration on page 41 of the cockatoo pattern shows the reverse-etch appearance. Compare it to the toucan illustration to its left.

The line in the middle of the page will coincide with the edge of the page when you line up the corner designs with the side patterns in the middle of the page (edge A to edge B or edge C to edge D).

B

A

C

D

On very large glass or mirror projects, these patterns can be used as the top, bottom and/or sides in conjunction with the corner designs on page 28.

To cut circles or rounded corners freehand requires much practice. Some art stores carry knife blades that fit into compasses. A few layers of masking tape can be stuck on top of the resist to hold the tip of the compass and keep it from slipping and scratching the glass or resist. The edges A and B and edges C and D can be aligned using the line in the middle of the page (see page 48).

These corner designs were blasted on the backside of the mirror on the front cover. The mirror was then resilvered with silver-leaf spray on the sandblasted areas.

Etching the black areas in the upper illustration will give you a glass or mirror with a clear center. Etching the black areas in the lower illustration will produce a window for privacy.

This pattern can be used in conjunction with the one on page 56. When used together, they can accommodate any size window, door or mirror. For mirrors, etch the areas shown in black in the illustration.

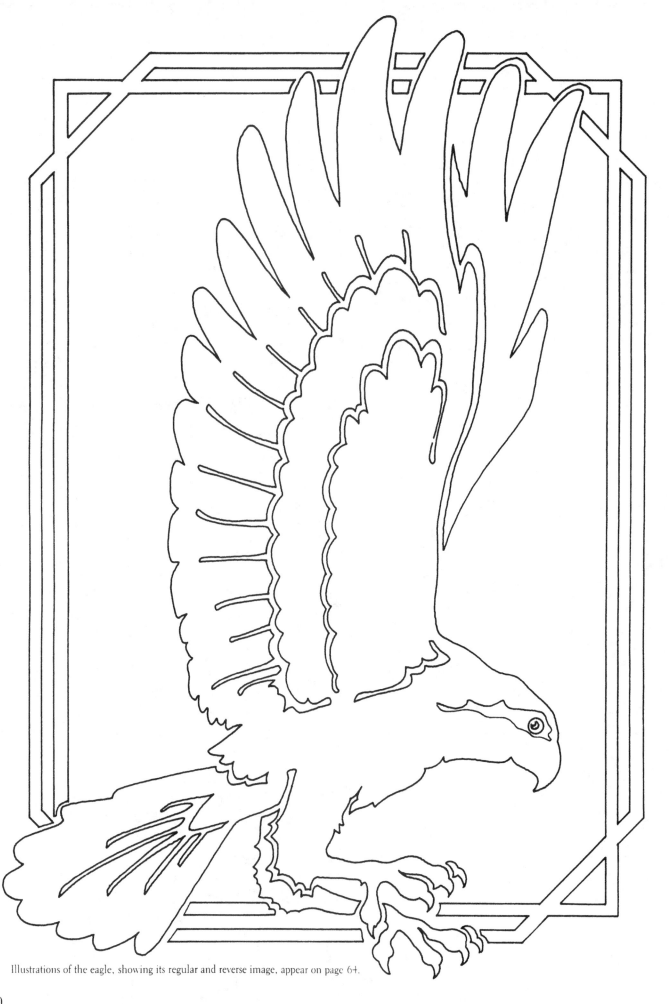

Illustrations of the eagle, showing its regular and reverse image, appear on page 64.

Regular and reverse-image illustrations of the two fish patterns appear on page 64. An illustration of the stars-and-stripes eagle appears on page 2.

Regular and reverse image illustrations of the patterns on page 60 and the top of page 61.